MINUTE-BY-MINUTE ACCOUNT OF JANUARY 6 2021

UNITED STATE OF AMERICA

A TRUE ACCOUNT OF EVENTS.

DAVID GOMADZA

www.twofuture.world

Minute-by-minute account of January 6 2021 united state of America

A true account of events.

Copyright © 2024 David Gomadza

All rights reserved.

PAPERBACK ISBN: 9798332099106

DEDICATION

To a better future.

CONTENTS

Minute-by-minute account of January 6 2021 united state of America

A true account of events.

Minute-by-minute account of January 6 2021 united state of America

A true account of events.

MINUTE-BY-MINUTE ACCOUNT OF

JANUARY 6 2021

UNITED STATE OF AMERICA

A TRUE ACCOUNT OF EVENTS.

ACKNOWLEDGMENTS

Tomorrow's World Order

BACKGROUND INFORMATION

January 6
United States Capitol attack

On January 6, 2021, the United States Capitol Building in Washington, D.C., was attacked by a mob[34][35][36] of supporters of then-U.S. president Donald Trump, two months after his defeat in the 2020 presidential election. They sought to keep Trump in power by occupying the Capitol and preventing a joint session of Congress counting the Electoral College votes to formalize the victory of President-elect Joe Biden. The attack was ultimately unsuccessful in preventing the certification of the election results. According to the bipartisan House select committee that investigated the incident, the attack was the culmination of a seven-part plan by Trump to overturn the election.[37][38] Within 36 hours, five people died: one was shot by Capitol Police, another died of a drug overdose, and three died of natural causes, including a police officer.[c][29][39] Many people were injured, including 174 police officers. Four officers who responded to the attack died by suicide within seven months.[30] Damages caused by attackers exceeded $2.7 million.[40]

MINUTE-BY-MINUTE ACCOUNT OF JANUARY 6 2021 UNITED STATE OF AMERICA

A TRUE ACCOUNT OF EVENTS.

Mr. trump tomorrow I will show you how to behave but you have to see what's in store for you talking about Joe Biden after finding out that fbi rigged last election to make Joe Biden win by asking employees to say if I were you who would you vote for then they sent 3.5billion messages to Americans who would have voted trump to change unless they are like trump after first calling him a wiz kinda hooligan message received from 823868789012385 fbi secret number hi I am wiz kinda hooligan would you vote for me of I was a kinda wiz kinda hooligan be serious I kinda need you right now but you kinda vote some foreign great guy and push your own to the sides that's kinda of saying give us a makeup to who we are you said as we are now you saw a great guy now kinda wiz hooligan then you drool billions what billions stolen fbi know ask for asert money sent to trigger shenanigans but taken and confiscated then distributed among those who found out what this account is used for to maim and kill innocent people 8 million used on 911 to represent the American dream without this we are so weak hence for him to come we must keep provoking his rage but who wants a war we just want gudo only all this is all a lie gudo is the right to everything on earth God understand do you know if I can then you vote for me then I will gudo all you when time comes gudo gudo gudo x0 now if I can explain they all want to end this country and shred it tomorrow Jan 6 all are waiting to riot because they want trump in power but we can't allow that in fact if we do then we lose face and the value of the gudo will change as well because they will go after the Asian who are rich and will present them with serious money that I would wizii hooligan checking out if we ask what can be this is the answer

What is to be of rioters and peace they all will be sent to jail but we will still be there if we ask what could be of those who want to

Minute-by-minute account of January 6 2021 united state of America

A true account of events.

disturb the peace this is the answer they will be charged and be sent to prison

Donald trump I can't think of anything else than that the election was stolen this really upsets me I believe as I am hearing that the wiz kid hooligan has been going on just before the vote if we are to ask what could be of American politics then this is the answer we could be out of politics but we didn't lose we won but they threatened everyone the day before the election with gudo because no one knows what it is this socks that ducks so what can be done about politics like this boycott so that it won't happen again if it is to be repeated then the constitution says you must revenge on second time so that freedom to vote is guaranteed but how can I revenge in situations like this you can start to prevent this happening according to the constitution by starting to confront constitution section 8 of the how to deter a rigging of the results you must confront brutally the other party in this way so that the rigging stops there is nothing so upsetting to the American people than the rigging of elections either by foreign parties or by local militia but worse if it's the fbi that means under your rights in the constitution you must confront the other side in such a way it stops the everyday life but without bloodshed you are entitled to defend your rights and preserve the constitution this means defending the freedom to vote what they did is threaten likely voters of you and demand they listen or else even if that's not exactly they said everyone is saying the use of this word gudo frightened them because it is synonymous with the word judo threatens to suffocate another person in sleep especially that the message was sent all as a batch at 03.48am Florida time on 06 January now if one is to ask what can be of rigging politics then this is the answer people went on to be killed later on now if we Ask what can be of Americans with rigged politics then they cant be of good to anyone the reason why America stands out is the fact that it can be trusted by anyone on earth to fair but they can be tricking bastards here and there but the truth remains the same there can never be a free and fair America unless issues of vote rigging are confronted front head without fear of jail or anything because if this is not done since it's a two way system then this will be repeated and to discourage this we must make sure that the first time there is proof then the rights engraved in the constitution must be upheld if rigging is the fine

Minute-by-minute account of January 6 2021 united state of America

A true account of events.

judge then riot of the kind never seen before must ensue this is because politics is different from business where one can fake documents and gain a competitive advantage in politics we can never rig elections just because the opponent rig business deals this is a recipe for disaster we the people in the constitution means we the people and will forever never mean the fbi or the current president as such tomorrow must be a day in which the rights of the people must be held this is because a country with a rigging election is not a fair or just country but a renegade country that is going to get everything trashed on day this is because if not God then someone will see sense and ask for a remote that is fair and right in the eyes of Justice that means that if we look at this case then we can conclude that if this is to happen again then there will never be an American constitution again because if we are to ask what can be of politics and vote rigging then this is a recipe for disaster that can't be tolerated but one that must be stopped with immediate effect I can't stress how important this is but acting is your duty as the opponent to protect the American constitution but its also deliberate so that they charge you for an insurrection which they will but if you are to fall is not great to fall as the great leader who defended the constitution or the whimsy guy who saved his arse and let vote rigging perpetuate so I ask is there a way I know what else I can do without the insurrection because the charges can get me out of politics if God is not there to protect me I swear if God is to appear and tell the truth I would give him anything he want but today is a make or break for America if I sleep I will go down as the whimsy crying boy whose wife got ravaged when he was there or the great defender of Justice but what can be of trump without politics and out of jail then he can be a great leader but with damaged reputation because to sleep today when they expect an insurrection will make them bring your case about forging papers to the front and demand that you surrender quickly by their predictions by January 2023 you will be in jail serving 20 years of business document forging that alone is enough to put you out of politics they want you out for 4 years anything along that time frame is enough to do everything they want so this is how to handle the insurrection like this without incriminating yourself go to the park where there is green life and don't use any papers or smile say I know what happened today is unfair but we can always defend the

Minute-by-minute account of January 6 2021 united state of America

A true account of events.

constitution from vote rigging so that this won't happen again in the interest of free and fair election if we are to ask what can be of American politics that without the free and fair part then this is the answer the election can be rigid again and again because the first rigging that is not addressed will continue since it is not addressed and the only way to address this is to ask for God to intervene because there is no one out there who can tell as it is than God God knows everything he will be able to tell as it is this case is also to test the existence of God because if we are to ask who on earth can know everything from both sides then there is none but God knows everything if God knows what they did then he will condemn it because this is what is in the constitution he helped to write now if God is just and want the American people to know the truth then he would tell everyone the truth that the people of America deserve better than the rigging of votes going on at the moment if the American people are to accept mediocre politics then they will support the current leader but as far as free and fair politics is concerned the current state has become intolerable if the state be can vote rig then what about the next election they will ballot rig which is worse because these things happen in stages once you vote rig and nothing is done then the next thing is to ballot rig which is actually difficult to prove if vote rigging can't be controlled then ballot rigging is the next if not dealt with the assassination of the president is the next step and all this is in the constitution where a president was assassinated by the fbi because he failed to obey the rules of the constitution and choose to stay in power it does not work that if but the other side decides to take you out with an insurrection to secure his place then you cant do nothing if you do its at your own risk this is because if you are to not fight then they will end it with an assassination by the fbi according to the rules and regulation of the constitution in the president's cabinet that accompanies the normal constitution but only for the president of the country which the fbi has a copy if a leader chickens out and fail to comply with the demands then the other secretive constitution gives rights to the fbi to correct the situation so its either you face Joe Biden now or the fbi later on

Miles away I know what happened tonight someone has just stepped up the process of initiating an insurrection by sending a whispering

Minute-by-minute account of January 6 2021 united state of America

A true account of events.

text message that says wiz kid hooligan is out and about this is within the constitution to trigger an insurrection and end his political career but unfairly because the current president has chickened out already but is still in the driver's seat and what he must do is to make his opponent insurrection if he does not then this is exactly what is going to happen
1. He will be charged with starting an insurrection
2. He will be tried in front of everyone
3. He will be sentenced to 20 years in jail there is no way to choose otherwise the secretive constitution says that he must be given 20 years no matter what
4. He will be charged for using fake documents but here there is an express mandate that says this person must be held in the country now just waiting for the 20 year term guaranteed there is nothing else that can be done but a straight 20 with no judge or anyone else to appeal to as this is part of the constitution but if we look at this we will see that if we are to ask what could be then this is the case we will see that to stand and survive all this the only way is to give up the presidency but cleverly now you can simple start your business again then then come back into politics but at a cost now they have to make everything public and charge you for forging documents even though it was a legal practice then then tell everyone that how can you stand for the presidency meaning automatic disqualification but with merit because you will say politics is not running a business then he will use insurrection to try and stop you but now you will have found fame again then come and do the same like him only that this don't get out because if this does fbi will and must shot you in public and national television like jfk this is exactly what happened and failed to address all the queries they are presenting to you they are asking 8 questions
1. Do you like rigged elections why he ask because he has incrementing information about your business deals Donald trump is a forgery what do you say it was the way business was conducted then all these are issues in the early 1970s nothing recent say Joe you are old
2. Donald do you like my daughter or to give me yours because I have information you want them young Joe check all your videos kissing children oh Donald it's because I never had a girl and I feel

Minute-by-minute account of January 6 2021 united state of America

A true account of events.

real affectionate give up
3. Are you a sissy boy because the decisions you are to make require guts and big balls we don't want good looking presidents who don't kill others if we stop now what will the world say about the ones before you that's not the American dream we stand with everything
4. How can you ask about justice when you are accused of bad things throughout history we have some people of color who speak bad about you do you stand for the American people or by your German roots if so I must take you out don't forget I was a soldier
5. You love Yahweh God but you don't act Yahweh you gave your daughter to a Jewish billionaire why didn't you let her chose because choosing for herself is the American way what's your answer I can't answer that
6. If you win will you rid votes like I tried to do I am not you
7. If I let you stand again will you let me win again without an insurrection as at the start but you charged me with an insurrection but that's not an insurrection that just the disturbing of peace nothing fancy about that because since business man don't understand how an insurrection is I will show you how to handle an insurrection is to put you away for 20 years
8. If I sent you to prison for 20 years what would you do I will pray to God to answer me and say you have been defrauded kill Joe Biden right now but you will be dead

As it happens.
Jan 6 2022 00.00 am president's office if I have to then I must but then and dropped the receiver down and cursed what can be done at this hour surely at my age I think somethings you ought to ignore says Biden but hoping someone is listening then gets out and celebrate then goes out
00.01 trump gets up and heard huge knocks at the door and sits what can be of today and what more important than my beautiful Mel sir the world is on fire they need you already can't they wait until the offices are open I can't stand the way Joe does things I am older but he is old
00.02 town square New York city the organizer listen up you all must bear with me for no one has got up yet otherwise the police would be here according to the constitution but we must be steadfast
00.03 Whitehouse sir there are huge gatherings in town square

Minute-by-minute account of January 6 2021 united state of America

A true account of events.

something to be worried about no sir only that you must know as per constitution of the United States when ever there is a huge gathering in the town square at 00.00am it could be an insurrection happening the very next day to warn and prepare you okay who insurrection against Joe Biden trump whimsy trump but you said he will chicken out and run away frustrated walks out

00.08 I have a dream the election has been rigid and as such we must start an insurrection how can I receive a wiz hooligan kid text messages that talked for exactly 22 seconds then fades into sleep until 8 minutes then stops?

00.10 if I can then what can stop me? The president? You mean rigging Joe?

00.11. If he can rig the election then he can rig the ballot we can't allow that as such we must act and fast

00.12 if someone can tell me what's going on in town square is that a signal for a pending insurrection police officer acetopmn meaning sornp

00.13 can we see what has been happening pointing at the screen then someone reminds but nothing just a crowd

00.14 if we can we must can but what about trump himself what is his stance does he support or want to be a wimpy trump someone warn him this is what happened to jfk and was shot so if he don't support now we know he will be shot by the fbi

00.15 I can't be shot what for a business man like me I don't think so maybe I should have stated out of business they all say I got out started by Joe without schooling at all he is costing me millions maybe count my cost and get out peacefully before this gets bad

00.16 I want trump to understand me very clearly all this that has been going on is bullshit he must give me the respect I have as the president of the country even if fbi helped me I don't care really I won that what counts that means that he has issues with other people so none of my business

00.17 if we can't stop this then what we must go into contingency planning right now

Pc adertoperstuvw meaning atorstup who said the world is starting to get interested I saw this on telly and said which part of Europe this is happening then saw the flag and said oh my God it's on our soil I waited for something like this all my life if I have to be out there I

Minute-by-minute account of January 6 2021 united state of America

A true account of events.

have to but we must ask ourselves a lot of questions about Justice and free elections I think this part has been neglected

00.18 if we can we must stop this insurrection I swear it won't look good on me if people realised trump can fight me then I am in deep trouble how can I look all those who were there when I call him whimsy trump he frowned and cursed but smiled

00.19 I want support right now left wing do you read over pc aseroy on the leftwing of the town square help I say he shouted

00.20 I can but this has nothing to do with me I just got woken up but if I knew I can tell but nothing to say look if you want answers as crooked Joe
for a change okay

00.21 if we ask what can be of insurrection and justice they all will be beaten and be brought before the court and sent to jail there is no one who has insurrection and left but go to the court be charged and be sent to jail

00.22 if I can then I can but My hands are tied look at the time test but if you were in the white house then you will be responding so do as that we can leave Joe Biden alone to this you also must take part the preliminary findings are that they are your people

00.23 I will let you know when I arrive on my way there right now pc tyuse

00.24 I have been near the scene its hard but I can always call for back up

00.25 I can but where are the others is this a stunt because it's not funny the pressured nearly busted my lungs I can't breathe properly what is long ago hello anyone read
Notes long ago is initiating of death in humans and other terrestrial creatures but it does not necessarily mean death but after being calculate it will remain that forever meaning the longer you get the more likely you will leave on earth

00.26 I will if we can but we must also know what can be of situations like this pc uareb at town square dreading the crowds as they started to move towards town centre to government buildings then calls for backup

00.27 what had been said about this situation has president trump been notified you fool Joe Biden is president I am not a fool this is happening because they rigged the election even if that was a small

Minute-by-minute account of January 6 2021 united state of America

A true account of events.

number of people to change results why do it the constitution clearly says even 1 can trigger an insurrection do you think all these people are fools they are being paid by trump but without the knowledge of the people otherwise I don't see it why insurrection for 3.5 only these should have run into 100ds but I think they just want to make noise right if you can then what can you do? I would arrest trump if they know he is arrested then nothing like this will happen ever again if we ask what can be of you then this is the answer if we are to look at this case trump is supposed to appear on national television and say I can if you can but you all must go home right now this is not what we do but it's not also the right way to stop it we must respect the wishes of the people who voted and accept it as it is goodnight then he will avert an insurrection and they all loved behind the scene and said it will be easy to get all arrested and fill all jails that's 12% bonuses and clapped hands

00.27 if we can then we must always protect the president I mean the current president who trump or Joe biden Joe biden but trump is the current president the election has put Joe Biden never mind these comments by these wishful thinkers are we are wishful thinkers right

00.28 I will but how are you getting home tonight I will give you a lift we can talk as we go leave your car I can drive you today no thanks if it's more than an insurrection what would I do without a car

00.29 I can but I need time I have pains in my belly something ruptured I could die you know don't be silly we can handle pressure you were not even here so how can you say that you think this is the case I just know

00.30 Mr trump this is why this gcsa has happened meaning the go cause some announcement they all laughed

00.31 Biden conference hall I want you all to know that we can contain the pressure and thwart trump in his plans to take over the city I promise you he will fail reporter Mr. president what can you do to stop this from escalating asked New York times reporter

00.32 we can do what we can but trump is stupid to think he can take Whitehouse by force I will send more back up to stop him

00.33 if we can then we can always be prepared and tonight is no less so be rest assured we can tackle and address all this fast than you have expected as we were training

00.34 we can always stay vigilant but what can be done to quell all

Minute-by-minute account of January 6 2021 united state of America

A true account of events.

this insurrection

00.35 we can always be prepared and ask what can be done but hope it's what we want also

00.36 if I can then this is what I want to be able to say I did my best to stop this in my powers
But it just wasn't enough pc omnpt giving a speech just near trafalgar Square

00.37 I can ask for help right now it's better than to be killed for trump help we need reinforcing at right back side pc tormn

00.38 if we can please cover the centre so the perrifycare observed pc Nordstrom

00.39 we can if you can but we need urgent help at back centre over does anyone read cursed

00.40 if you heard clearly there is an insurrection in town square are you listening melamine what's wrong my love I am upset you chose to fight and compete with Joe Biden everytime you do that you lose image leave Whitehouse we have trump tower then what we do after trump tower in old age

00.41 I want another kid a boy again so let's go and make another all this insurrection is a trick to spill all dirty about you before we met but I don't care I chose us over them okay Whitehouse was the dream come true American dream even better when I came here but we enjoyed that now think about running the world that's next I want from you okay leave Joe Biden it's everyone you can't fight Russia so you will be out better by yourself then to be forced out like a school boy man would walk away because the target is 500 000 Ukrainians dead can you do that I ask you as your wife

00.42 I want you to know I will never kill another human being even in the past I never killed anyone I love you okay but I can't sleep when there is an insurrection can I yes perfectly we can make the best love all waiting for me while we do another dream so make me fulfill that one first I promise to but if a man sleeps when there is a war he will die in sleep

00.43 if I can then I can buy you must also ask what could be of this insurrection okay what could be of this insurrection it could be a real life changing opportunity to stand for freedom of election and prove to the world that justice can be done even by a businessman what they are saying is this that a businessman cannot take office and do a

Minute-by-minute account of January 6 2021 united state of America

A true account of events.

good job because to protect the country you must cheat and kill as well but you are too honest to kill even though you are smart businesslike leadership wise you are dump because you are going to reveal secrets that will cause the country to be destroyed I don't get it what can he possible do what I can't do better can you kill innocent women and children because the next phase involve that no I can't do that why do we have to kill women and children for 0.44 what the most strongest country on earth why do we need this we need a war with Russia using a proxy what no russia China you idiots I can fight China Russia then what I do if they target my wife's family she is not Russian why he doubt questions himself

00.45 if we ask what can be of usa and China this is the answer China and USA can never be in the same war or in the opposite sides forever or else that will be the end of usa as a superpower and if we ask what can be of Russia and usa they must fight now offload all weapons to Ukrainian then start all over again to boost sales just after elections making whoever is in power the real business leader as sales and demand will exponentially rise but she is Ukrainian and has Russian relatives so better quit the job so that they spare all or get the targeted to match Joe Biden I can't either get out

00.46 I can but you must be prepared to sacrifice for your own country I can and no many has sacrificed a lot than me my wife my son and possibly my daughter she was pregnant yes I mean kill others to sell weapons no I can't sorry then you say that they were killed to avenge those you killed if that is the case then give to trump to target his own inlaws I'm old but not stupid okay what if Americans don't fight but Ukrainians fight them you mean Russian and Ukrainians yes if that's the case with no blood on my hands then I am in

00.48 he is in so trump must be done with but slowly if we do it fast everyone will suspect that it's meddling in politics and nothing to do with the feud between the two so ring the fbi and say trump resigned automatically they will know what this means

00.49 if we wait too long everyone will be here before we break in what's taking too long

00.50 what is happening in town Square as if they are waiting to attack let's go and see asmot and atqers

00.51 i know what can be must be but if we are to then what? Pc

Minute-by-minute account of January 6 2021 united state of America

A true account of events.

suern before being kicked in the head then stabbed upon resulting in death long ago started at 00.51 and lasted 3 seconds before he died of suffocation
Notes he is the one injured during the first push splitting his intestines resulting in oxygen leak then died at 00.54
00.52 if I can then you can but you must admit this isn't for you so that we make things easy and fast I have an asm too mine actually better because it told me that you come is planning to get 500000 Ukrainian women women and children killed for weapons sales but I don't understand why this has to be 500000 if none dies can you not sell the weapons I can answer nonsense questions but you can so how many do you prefer to kill none outright my wife is from these areas so nothing maybe Joe should take the job if it involves deaths of women and children he already did so what that means for you is the fact that to keep you quiet is to take you instead to die for the crimes he is going to commit if you had accepted we would have killed him he had agreed that means the chicken just like jfk refusing to do what Nixon did will be blasted by fbi and or 20 years without anyone saying anything I can't die for country if I knew God was listening to your shit talk I would personally recommend you be sacked in fact I will sack you before I left office and when God comes we can all judge you for sacrificing women and children for a pay check you can't fire me trump as things are by midday tomorrow as in jfk you will be toast and if I fire you first then no one knows meaning you pushing all this nonsense America is great not because it kills women and children but because it respects women and children they all laughed what school did you go to don't start with I am still president you have no respect for me or the presidency I love the presidency if you sack me then I will run as independent ah so that what you want yes now tell me what you want I want to remain president but without war with Russia but China okay you asked and I have told you
00.53 I can but ask you what is going on give me your leader so we start negotiations okay nothing to negotiate with vote riggers the constitution stipulates that once that is done then we must immediate start an insurrection or be sent to jail he laughed no I mean be sent to jail first then start an insurrection in that case you are all under arrest they tricked you to get rid of all you hooligans don't you know the

Minute-by-minute account of January 6 2021 united state of America

A true account of events.

hooligan wiz kid has been visiting people in their sleep you dump asrses you do exactly that you are not supposed to do if you were smart this is how you would handle the situation admit you are a hooligan prone to violence then stay at home because the wiz kid had told people that whisper to people who so that we get rid of all those who are likely to resurrect after elections and document them then wait to see what trump can do without his entrouge of trouble makers as a security precaution then he said do you know that they are planning to kill 500000 Ukrainians if the war started bodies of which will reduce their debt to the usa by hundred thousand dollars but how when they donate billions yes but read the small print maximum donation in cash is 5 billion dollars I said 100billion dollars profit or savings the other donations are to do with military gear weapons to offload literally all so that after the next election the economy booms exponentially like after the Nixon years are you made take us back to the sixty why surely killing women and children is not justified so we must keep insurrection then it shout not be an insurrection but a disgruntlement plan therefore illegal and must be arrested no its an insurrection you can't arrest us who talked about women and children before this

00.54 I can but My hands are tied if I can then I can but you must be clear what you need doing we are clear reduce population by 500000 so if we loan them they will be able to reduce the money they owe us already in billions if it wasn't for this we could have ignored both but now we can see how bad this is we have to change leadership from Russia lover to Russia hater so this is what this is all about I see then take Joe Biden I will still fight thought but how can I lie to my wife but she told me but just didn't sink in now it makes sense

00.55 if we keep going on like this someone will be killed one office died already see why I keep saying I must arrest all of you then insurrection in court and instantly he got punched and stumbled upon by others and long ago started at 00.58 and died at 00.59 no any oxygen detected in his body to continue long ago message received by his internal organs as measured by Yahweh's hologram that measures all statistics when a human being dies and sends a copy to ya as a send.ya but in reverse meaning ya.send david gomadza you sent message to yourself ...davidgomadza is yahweh...nothing damaged but things have improved the bestest for the past 48 years

Minute-by-minute account of January 6 2021 united state of America

A true account of events.

your long ago beats all gods even Yahweh's and stands at 8908367890 billion years who are you I am Yahweh's representative on earth Praise Oh Yahweh for humans have lived more than the gods

00.56 I can if you are not but only because you are forcing me since trump refused this job then either admit you are forcing the president of the United state to kill women and children so I am in good books with God or I kill trump and say he forced me to kill those women and children your choice right now you did not give me time to think comes you will die young if you mess up with me I know trump sacked you already that is my job I an not flattered by your threats okay my son died and I won't hesitate to kill you okay I can fucken blast you ugly mothersucken trash I fed up I fought a real war against the might men not trash my name as having blood of Killers I mean of women and children I can refuse as trump then your dream dies and someone out there will do that for this job

So your choice you have 3 minutes or I am out to give to someone else fast I chance we are doing you a favour at your age who is afraid of dying this is stupid I can't me too all these threats for 38000 dollars when this is how you crooked steal billions from the American people then I refuse too so Joe Biden get out you are not president if you touch me I will confess I am gay and these single men keep asking me for sake you and your shaking but I am not that shit I have Jill you say that again I will okay maybe you are right that means when I pressure trump you must not interfere if you interfere then it's your neck because I will admit you are doing this for billions if money at the expense of how many again 500000 Mr. new president give me a hug fuck off so you refused my offer bye and he rescued out but cried outside when he found out that trumped had sacked him without pay to fix the bastard

00.56 if I Ask what has been going on then the war is about to happen in Russia what is left is for the American public to be told to expect another 911 so that when this comes out then there won't be any issue the president will simply say I told them already that means the all clear from everyone if we ask what can be of the future and war then this is the answer the war can be something that can solve all American problems but the cost is way huge American through the world Bank has imposed strict rules where it funds its interests

Minute-by-minute account of January 6 2021 united state of America

A true account of events.

and this has meant the killings of innocent women and children all that so that the country is in a position to repay the loan back does that not sound too strict because women and children must be valued
00.57 it matters not because even God benefit from their deaths through the gaining of the souls why God need souls they save information inside dead souls heads I don't believe this who told you this I am Jewish God punishes women and children Killers in that case you got me put me in jail he laughed but zelensky did not see the amusement part
00.57 I can't even ask what has been because now it start skipping that part meaning we are out of the Whitehouse it was a great pleasure but the dream is over and sat down in the chair
00.58 if I can then I will but comey push so hard you can't tell who is the president I want him fired today when offices open
00.59 Mr. new president you have just taken over and democratically elected what can you say about all this I am excited finally the dream is here for us to enjoy okay I better go and tell fox we finally did it before the fake insurrection trump is whimsy I can believe he split did he not know all the drills when we were young trumps answer I was not born in this country
01.00 if I Ask what can be of trump and his family this is the answer trump will pack tomorrow to trump tower or even to prison because he has not shown power if he does not appear then he is finished he must be seen once on national television of his choice but he attacks everyone of them he don't believe in all these stupid drills look what they made you do you won free and fair why did you send the text they want it to look like they helped you so they humiliate you who are you talking about the national hospital service am I sick no you just don't know what they do so you look like a laughing stock but you won nice and fair there are rumors you sent a message after elections telling people that one day you might strangle them in their sleep he laughed but how see how shaky my hands have become If I don't do something about this then I am going to let culprits walk free I don't think so
01.01 if I am honesty the world want to see what America can do in regard to free elections and look what crazy Joe is saying this must stop but he gets worse he literally does the opposite but it's the American way only this time he went too far sending the wiz kid

Minute-by-minute account of January 6 2021 united state of America

A true account of events.

hooligan I wish I knew all this but I was not born here I was born in another great country only that it stood for the wrong reasons but I love being American did you say I was born in another great country I mean my father I always repeat what he used to tell us when we were growing up do you know it's forgery to pretend to be born in this country when you were born in another country I was born here in New Orleans so there you go it's true don't listen they cause unnecessary troubles in times like this but we must all stand together as one if we are to ask what can be of the presidency role under Biden this is the answer he will be so sacred of trump enough to put him behind bars in January 2025 if trump does not take action what action does trump take in this situation he must stop the insurrection but cleverly they planned one of your aides to write for you what to say just to diminish your authority if you read all he wrote then you are dead because he is literally admitting that you sent all to cause not an insurrection but hooliganism as such a renegade and Biden will use the constitution under renegade laws to put you in prison for straight 20 years his target there are rumors that to keep you distracted the fbi will initiate criminal charges against Biden son if you say bad things about him he will ask for straight 20 by January 2025 and death in your cell by December 2026 by code 823848678902858786780 if we look at the history of these kinds of challenges from Ibrahim Lincoln to jfk the presented targeted to die died on the same day as planned the reason being that he owns so much property that the other need to give everyone involved a 5% cut of the value at sale amounting to 75% of and him getting either his son free or the 20% with always the 5% unaccounted for often given to his wife in the case of jfk trump froze body temperature dropped to -2 degrees and he cried and one tear dropped down and said can this be stopped and by who then they all looked at each other and said only God can stop what has been initiated if he wants to he can tell exactly what happened and let the people decide how if he has the last say but no one ever spoke to God and lived that's why but someone can interpret for you that you have been sentenced to death on 17 January 2025 at exactly noon for betraying the United States by colluding with Russia just like jfk because we took their lands so if you are nice to them that means you will end up getting everyone killed so Joe Biden is in a position to attack Russian is the

Minute-by-minute account of January 6 2021 united state of America

A true account of events.

only true American president trump just like jfk will get us be destroyed by Russia one day so everyone refused you even your own wife

01.02 if I can then we all can but ask what can be of this country without the trumps the country can be safe again trump is a great business man but a weak politician who will not shed blood throughout his years as president and then leave a lot of questions to be answered why if he can do his presidency without shading blood why not has ever done it that will be the greatest challenge a test that can see all former presidency be indicted and be sent to prison something more likely in the future there are predictions Joe Biden will be the last of those war leaders so we need to give him a great sending without trump reminding him how things will be in the future just like Lindon Johnson request trump is likely to get short on January 17 at noon 2025 as the date picked by the house of representative fir trumps death but on conditions

1. If he live the country he will be buying himself time
2. If convinced on any charges that means will never leave like jfk
3. If he admits fraud and paying for information then he is prone to be short by fbi
4. If he denies it and still get found guilty an assassin will be summoned to kill him
5. If he can then ask what can he do then we check with the secret constitution he can ask God for help has he asked God for help many times God help me die old age I refused to kill women and children so help me God what can God do he can tell the truth write a book and publish it this is also one of the reason why this is done to find if God exist what they do is to switch off everything that can record and send signals to Yahweh as part of all drills then use the drill information to cover fir this one when people know when this happened after 17th January 2025 then the drill information is the one used but if it's God then he will know what happened so again this is also for God if he is there he will tell us what happened not us telling him what happened

01.03 I want to get in open the door right now officer it's nit an insurrection so go away you brat horned devil with no shirt on camera someone quickly he is turning aggressive I am own my own please help okay just come and help us I can here you you want it to

Minute-by-minute account of January 6 2021 united state of America

A true account of events.

look that we are hooligans because you know from the drills that if its an insurrection then we must perform a ritual you know the secret constitution read this he handed a copy and waited I have never seen this before none have seen this our copy only comes out when something like this happens but nothing happened from your point of view yes but from our point of view something happened if we go home then they are going to kill someone who did not grow up here only because if that because he doesn't know all this just like jfk who grew up on England who said about killing trump he is refusing to exit he agreed that is what they are calling treason fbi confessed he is facing treason charges hidden as fraud charges so that he does not react like he would do under normal circumstances what normal circumstances if he went to a president would he had refused to kill women and children for power do you think that he is to die for refusing yes if he does die then what then how can he keep quiet about about intend to kill 500000 Ukrainians what if the war started in less than 4 weeks then 500000 dies then what but its under presidential secrets so covered but if he let's out any of that after he left then maybe but I think if he survives this then he will be the first and the fbi will be harsh with trump so that Biden ask for his death instead if 20 years in prison but to be shot on national television and at noon exactly so that by 13.00 his body will be in hell as in the case of jfk for ever never to speak to Yahweh God because if allowed to do then God will save him and send him to heaven where he will live forever rather than wait in hell for end of days with the possibility of having sex

01.04 if I can say something today has been a day of learning okay I believe it's a real constitution and since I am from India I discover that I might not know anything deeper than this see I cooperate for your freedoms of election and voting but I ask a favour let this be peaceful then I can keep my job okay what your name if you ask me then I have to ask yours too what you prefer anything I am jabltet Singh then he started singing then he said I lied I can't give you my name because insurrection is not a game of cat and mouse as it can be a matter if life and death but because I am not doing anything out of the constitution my name is aerot amnopt meaning Oscar so let us in we just walk inside parliament slowly like a bull and out maximum 8 minutes then he said all these for 8 minutes yes if they

Minute-by-minute account of January 6 2021 united state of America

A true account of events.

send trump to abyss we sent them there too too they laughed and they entered slowly pointing as if picking out people the walked out within 7 minutes as he kept the count down on as the leader then left and said I thank you for trusting me you actually saved by life we can be friends he agreed and they left and cried when he heard 3 police officers were crushed to death and said he had no shirt I asked him to turn around search for weapons etc he complied with my requests and left so I see no reason to arrest him then the other said he is the leader 3 officers lost their lives today who should we arrest then he left and threw the badge on the floor

01.05 I can but if you can then tell me why the insurrection is still going on and why am I hearing that 3 police officers have died who killed them trump looked lost and said is this a set up and slammed the receiver

01.06 I can but you can always count on me to be there and to do a great job so tell me what can be of trump without Whitehouse he can start ripping the benefits of renovating trump tower after today he has a house better than trump tower to celebrate victory over Joe Biden who agreed to kill women and children which is actually said just to be in the Whitehouse but then said do you know it also means trumps death sentence to die after 1.25 years by 17 January 2025 just like jfk a repeat of jfk who refused to fight the soviet union instead choosing China now trump doing the exact mistake so what can be of trump after 17 January 2025 in hell waited to be screwed by the devil he chose fbi to blast him instead of an assassin but then fbi provide their own just like in the case of jfk where they provided their own Elvis chosen by Edgar j hoover

01.07 if I can then you can I had no idea American politics is full of traps I only said I rather be shot and die and everyone move on then they all said he chose the fbi but assassin might duck and you can walk free but fbi do it for free so you can offer them anything whereas an assassin can ask you for money and arrange you live the country what do you really want your own asm say you are not American by birth you fooled us once then leave okay so that you life is spared the reason why they were harsh with jfk is that he was British born in England then destroy everything before setting foot then when here get fake documents before asm he could fool people because who is clever enough to calculate and compute but now you

Minute-by-minute account of January 6 2021 united state of America

A true account of events.

need only ask the asm what is trumps nationality according to his brain scans which only it so far can read it will say based on his brain scan as at birth he was in asertop meaning city of Berlin at a hospital now changed with his own money called stuvertyop meaning isterton Berlin but whose birth records was vandalized just before trump registered to campaign for presidential elections then on live debate said I was born in another great country a code sent to him by pc asornt of Los Angeles police department 81238654867890284878902856 78 was sent to him what it does is replace his brain thoughts with his father's so that sometimes he honestly say things about him but speak as his own father 81238654867890284878902856 78 I convert thoughts from himself to his father's so that when he speaks as himself he say what his father used to say a code used by fbi to frame jfk who was a real American but whose documents were lost or hidden by the fbi

01.08 I can but there must some trust we must also be fair in politics I am tired of hearing all this bullshit that politics is a dirty game I came to clean it but look they put on the hooks me so be straight to the point I can but only if you can but then you gave up everything to Biden image what can do to you if 500000 people die in terms of compensation it's a way of pushing me out of politics if God finds out that I am killing g women and children for power I think he can kill me too but I thought about it why have bad reputation at the end of your life Joe Biden has no business he dies everything dies if I die which I will one day then then it means if I kill all these people their relatives will claim compensation from my family enough to collapse the business most are with me ..... has died but will stick with me but I can say for sure that killing women and children of others can get yours killed as well so I understand why they want Joe Biden he lost literally everything I feel for him only that this can't be used as an excuse to kill now this time of the World affairs when everyone is looking so I refuse to act that way but to become a business man again

01.09 I can go and ask what can be of the police and trump then this is the answer the police and trump will form partnerships to screw each forever they are tricking him that he need to prove all his business dealings so that he overlook some of the documents retrieval laws so that we can get him for stealing government

Minute-by-minute account of January 6 2021 united state of America

A true account of events.

property then turn everything into a circus until he resigns from politics for 4 years when he wants a come back then start again as if to clear him but now to fully charge him with treason that way we will have fulfilled the two requirements of document stealing as in jfk hiding documents in the school depository so that cases he is involved in don't looked at like the death of marlin manroe which the fbi suspected he had killed her by strangulation then sent her to heaven instead of to hell so that all genital organs are removed to cover his sex acts with her as such tramp can die as early as 17 January 2025 if he does not know how to handle accusations of theft instead he will be left open to be summoned again in mid 2024 and on the day jfk died for finally confirmation of treason charges
01.10 if we can then we can what can be of trump and the media after he resigned he will be out of the media
01.11 what can be of trump and the whitehouse he handed in today notice of eviction after losing the presidential votes squarely but after Biden being scared he will refuse to live the Whitehouse tricked his supporters to try too create a situation of hostage saying I am old and take precaution you put me in power so accept I can't understand if it's wrong and everything about me why did you not put him instead in power so accept my plan or wait next voting season okay who need this kind of hassle at my age that means trump still want to run for president not that the war is in its final years where he can say Biden hence Biden now aiming to do him the jfk which if successful will see him blasted on 17 January at 12.00 noon
01.12 if they can then we can if the police can set up trump and use illegal codes to tune how what he says sounds then we the people can do the same police officer in civilian clothes asotenop who said I can help take trump tower down for 5% then everyone started shouting
01.13 what can be of trump tower if convicted of the 20 year treason fellow reduced to death it will be demolished as over the years people were complaining about him targeting his uneconomical expensive tower with rooms for 5000 dollars per night for Saudi Arabians only who can afford it there might not last
01.14 what did I say about trump the mayor of New York I told you if trump is to stay clean that will make all look bad that Joe Biden will say you made me touch shit so you pay because if you had accepted none of this could have happened but still it was your fault

Minute-by-minute account of January 6 2021 united state of America

A true account of events.

hence the one to pay 20 years or die on 17 January 2025 at 12 noon exactly we Americans take seriously traitors even your wife can't stop this this time by threatening to ask Russia for help

01.15 if you are seriously about politics you must be prepared to shade blood of women and children I did you must as well others if you look good then everyone will start to ask why we can't do the same if you can that's unacceptable a lost my family what can I say is that your excuse no but these things happen but if we are to look at all this then we must also be prepared to shade the blood of others otherwise it's not politics if you are not serious you will go down he call me crazy but I am president the constitution states that a president no matter what can never be crazy otherwise he is not a present

01.16 if we were there what could be the reason for all this I think the world is losing 3 officers dead already in freaky accidents all dying of strangulation as if someone's hands were put on their necks if we look at these deaths the first office was only pushed in if we check if any codes were received then this is the only code received by him 83897890287678902849867821051 kill silently the strongest people on earth by bubbling all your lungs then remove all air that your body will act as if you have been strangled but has a simple antidote 878367890284 than remove its attachments it relies on its own network of things that are easily removed by this code 878367890284 making it safer in a flash if we check the other officer he was not attacked but he died too through a code 8928764838789028678902841836789028413678901 this code removes air from the lungs and trigger hard breathing that can imitate strangulation but again has a simple code that it attaches to is easily destroyed by code 089838764810 then if we ask what happened to him death is also by above code now if we look at what killed the third one then its the same as the second one now what are the sources of these gods the first was from this number 827678908326480 if we check this is the answer I am owned by Zack

who is fbi agent and entrusted in making Joe dance

All 3 codes came from him too

I am Zachariah stopemver I work for the digital agency Institute funded from the fbi asert account to deal with issues that can disturb

Minute-by-minute account of January 6 2021 united state of America

A true account of events.

the flow of things what do you mean you make Joe Biden dance his job is to kill women and children and to protect him is to make him look weaker then stronger after the war since its American war they died because of riots but we have proof you sent them 3 codes two identical and one different it's classified information about the codes
01.17 I will but then again you want to ask too much then refuse the answer what can be done and could be of the British interfering with American politics we can attack the whole country if we have to
01.18 what has happened during the evening that we don't know about looking at the cctv 3 died from strangulation or suffocation oh my God was it that serious replay what is going on who is behind this did they literally die or our own die they all looked at each other and all laughed and said police officer dying from suffocation without any contact at all so where are they they died real death and are I hell reception we check say officerasteroperomnopwhereareyounow.ya
I died for real they said it was only a drill I arrived at hell reception and Yahweh said you got killed by Zack one of you but partly works for fbi but this has nothing to do with fbi for his personal gratification current coordinates 08.9876483867890 and 28.7868789083 north of New York city in the woods hiding from fbi if we are to ask what can be of Zack then this man blackmail a lot of celebrities and even the president
01.19 I can see why it will be hard to let trump go in the end evertime he opens his mouth to complain the just kill someone and said add on trumps crimes but how can this end and when Rudy Gillian mayor of newyork
01.20 I'd we can then today is a sad day in American politics because trump got indicted he tried to change the politics if the day and got shot for that is there is not justice in American then where else on earth do you expect this to happen I want to go home and tell my wife we failed but trump stood him ground and got a standing ovation but that could also be the way he dies he must ask God for help in that now only God can clear his name but telling nothing but the truth but how you mean God coming down to write a book just for trump I don't see it why interrupt me when I am speaking to God pc steorpsters of London sctland yard
01.21 I know this is also about democracy but whose democracy

Minute-by-minute account of January 6 2021 united state of America

A true account of events.

American fight the middle east yet look how sad their lives are trying to kill this guy trump for standing up to democracy and the 1948 declaration of human rights that gives women and children rights to be not attacked by anyone

01.22 if I can then I can ask others to join to stop this madness but who is willing to die for trump but we can always defend democracy so today I resigned from the police force under bidden we have become his underwear to wear and change us as he pleased if I look at this case then I can say for sure that justice has been denied because what trump is saying among his friends is that they want to start a war with Russia with aim of removing 500000 Ukrainian women and children this is not just wrong but unlawful he realised that with this compensation culture this is to destroy him financially imagine 500000 women and children living their fathers and husband's it's your own death sentence

01.23 we can always ask what is everyone else doing about American politics the French say leave then alone they are looking for someone to accuses about starting election rigged so they start a war the Russians say they are full capacity and will involve us in a war with Ukraine and the Ukrainians say the American been good friends but why trump refused the presidency just because women and children this make no sense unless it's a war with Russia that's is going to kill women and children If we check this is likely but I don't see Russia attacking us unless but still makes sense sorry my English not good some explained me why trump refused the presidency and say Joe Biden can I have businesses and can't pay compensation zelensky

01.24 if I can I can but there is no justice in asking what can be when there is nothing to ask about trump chickened out and walked but did he walk or is another jfk in the making

01.25 I can if you can but you chickened out today but I will give you 20 or push for a jfk Biden upset after trump called him crazy

01.26 I was thinking I can but then I realised that they want to kill women and children but why and who will pay compensation in the future If they can clarify that maybe I will take the job but without written statement on this I will refuse because I am not afraid to die
...Joe Biden keeps saying he will give me 20 but from where and for what so I asked him today and he said I will teach you the American

Minute-by-minute account of January 6 2021 united state of America

A true account of events.

way you will listen when time comes but only when it really sink in but make no mistake anyone who call a president crazy I swear must die by a bullet to the head and aimed and trump took phone and he stopped
01.27 I could have been short but somehow he realised hoe bad his idea was and said go asterop after getting stopped during insurrection and said I am not part of all this I am coming from work then quickly flashed work wear and left
01.28 I killed a cop but without touching him something happened to him I was in front so I know no one touched him but he died he only said what is long ago
God I died I was killed by a mob but no one touched me I am pc aseortep mnopqrst real name adore stuvt I work for the Los Angeles leads department that supply information about presidential convicts who will serve jail time like president trump I mean former who refused a task to fight our enemies in russiah then think he can ever walk again on earth but secretly they have actually charged him with treason and will be shot on 17 January 2025 at noon unless God decides... unless you send help to help him but who is God of all of you is that one body with 7 heads oh 8 with a beautiful woman I take the woman that's disrespectful of my wife in that case you are challenging me but how did I know she is your wife attached on my left side meaning I and her are like these two couples sealed for eternity so that's 9 heads what about all theses 6 judges one messenger to write you write as well everything yes so now we have information about who killed you and how Zack a former fbi agent blackmail celebrities even president Biden killed you I cried he spoke like a human being and he knows even Joe Biden who else you know I questioned this thinking I am still alive he said Elon musk I cried and looked at myself then I only saw real human legs with no shoes floating but that's all a can see so I said where is my body look at look with so many hearts and where is mine he said imagine how humans die and everyone coming here with the same rating body this place wouldn't be this nice would it be then i realised I had died and he said you need enough rest go to hell reception and stay there forever so I said what about heaven they all loved and looked at the woman very beautiful and she looked down at my pants and everything fell off and she said got to heaven wait for me don't

Minute-by-minute account of January 6 2021 united state of America

A true account of events.

worry if you find someone you love everything will grow back again
01.29 I was about to ask what happened to the police officers when I received a report from the lab the toxicology report said he was strangled but without anyone touching him so I said whose ghost and when and said Donald j trump January 17 2025 with all his billions getting killed by a ......Joe Biden I swear be careful about the people you upset some use what you call them to send you to Jesus but I think he is too harsh on him because trump don't know the American way of living the country but once to fight for democracy this is in sane and live all these billions for Biden and your wife gets 10% no 5% the unaccounted portion that's harsh from the richest then the president the lower than jfk it hurts what happened to the American spirit of free elections and free speech I think he might survive this until 17 January hey Joe Biden can actually die first they all laughed if we ask what can be of us and them this is the answer the American way has always been free and fair but recently it had been anything but pc azertpt of newyork police department before he screamed and said I have seen a ghost and died.

Donald trump country of birth new Orleans usa I can figure out how they do this but they swap what my father said to make me switch back and forth if I find someone to tell me how these people are doing it I will pay him handsomely

There was no insurrection as far as the out of creation is concerned Joe Biden actually charged president trump with treason even though nothing he did falls along these lines he is waiting death and the person to shot him is or was there the one without a shirt he will be released on the 17 and get shot at at noon.

Can the treason charges be fought can he survive this if the world knows the truth he could be saved.

End of part one
Buy the next explosive minute by minute account of what happened on Jan the 6th

Minute-by-minute account of January 6 2021 united state of America

A true account of events.

Signed 3 July 2024

David Gomadza

President of Tomorrow's World Order

The First Global President of the World

Yahweh [God] Representative

ask.davidgomadzaauthorised.licensed.checkya.askya.ya

Signed

David Gomadza

President of Tomorrow's World Order

Also

Yahweh's Representative on earth

03 July 2024 21.48pm

Scotland

Minute-by-minute account of January 6 2021 united state of America

A true account of events.

TOMORROW'S WORLD ORDER'S PERSPECTIVES

…I found God…visit www.twofuture.world

THE CLAIM

www.twofuture.world/donate

ABOUT DAVID GOMADZA

visit www.twofuture.world

signed david gomadza
ask.davidgomadzaauthorised.licensed.checkya.askya.ya

03 July 2024 101.00 am

scotland
00447719210295
davidgomadza@hotmail.com
info@twofuture.world

Minute-by-minute account of January 6 2021 united state of America

A true account of events.

Minute-by-minute account of January 6 2021 united state of America

A true account of events.

Minute-by-minute account of January 6 2021 united state of America

A true account of events.

Minute-by-minute account of January 6 2021 united state of America

A true account of events.

Minute-by-minute account of January 6 2021 united state of America

A true account of events.

www.ingramcontent.com/pod-product-compliance
Lightning Source LLC
Chambersburg PA
CBHW030515220526
45464CB00006B/2807